TRIO
POETRY

ANGELA GREENE
OLIVER MARSHALL
PATRICK RAMSEY

THE
BLACKSTAFF
PRESS

BELFAST

ACKNOWLEDGEMENTS

Some of these poems have previously appeared in *An Múinteoir*, *Belfast Review*, *Clonmel Nationalist Supplement*, *Footnotes*, *Gown Literary Supplement*, *Honest Ulsterman*, *Irish Arts Review*, *Irish Press*, *Irish Times*, *Map-Makers' Colours* (Nu-Age Editions, Montreal), *North Dakota Review*, *Other Poetry*, *Poetry Wales*, *Rostrum*, *Salmon*, *Studies*, *Sunday Tribune*'s 'New Irish Writing', *Verse*; and broadcast on BBC Radio Ulster.

19/6/92

First published in 1990 by
The Blackstaff Press Limited
3 Galway Park, Dundonald, Belfast BT16 0AN, Northern Ireland
with the assistance of
The Arts Council of Northern Ireland

Typeset by Textflow Services Limited

Printed by The Guernsey Press Company Limited

British Library Cataloguing in Publication Data
Greene, Angela
Trio 6 poetry.
1. Poetry in English. Northern Irish writers, 1945–
Anthologies
I. Title II. Marshall, Oliver, *1948*– III. Ramsey, Patrick, *1962*–
821.9140809416

ISBN 0–85640–431–4

CONTENTS

ANGELA GREENE

Angela Greene was born in Dublin and currently lives in Drogheda, County Louth. Her work has been published in *Poetry Wales*, the *Honest Ulsterman*, *Irish Press* and *Sunday Tribune*. In 1988 she won the Patrick Kavanagh Award and in 1989 was short-listed for the *Sunday Tribune* Hennessy Literary Award.

DESTINY

Then her eyelids were the damson's bloom
and her cheeks were ripe.
Then her hair flossed umber shadows
down the sweep of her creamy nape,
and the tips of her lively hands shone
like peeled almonds.

Her blue dress and her snowy apron were crisp
and she sang as she worked,
deftly patient with those in her charge.

Then she got married, and in that free
and giddy twenties way
she sat astride their first motorbike.

Where apple blossom pollened the lanes
they tumbled their burning kisses
into waves of cool grass.

Then pregnant, again and again
her breasts
were the moist cambric of the midnight hours.

She rose early. To bake bread
and to launder by oil light;
or pulling the blinds for the sun's warm splash,
she worked
till those folded nights blotted her damp skin.

I was happy one day close in her milky scent
when he came home early;

3

my father, and the midwife in her navy coat,
and those soft eyes nudged me outdoors.

Through the clear glass, when I stood on tiptoe,
I saw her thighs
heaped like bruised poppies onto the white sheet.

I shush by that April window
till, in its searchings, her voice finds me out.
Its thin cries pierce me.
They sift down my blood like blown seed
from somewhere
                    far off.

THE LOST GARDEN

In here time waits.
Bees trade in the pollened air,
drugging the scented levels.
Fruit trees, roses and border pinks
lose their grip to a smother
of brambles and scutch –
a springy undergrowth made slithery
with cankered branch bits
and ginger leaves.

Red admirals are balletic,
embroidering nettle clumps
to marigolds. Along the hedge,
the white-faced elderflowers
flare in a dazzle of light,
and a thrush springs
to crack the seal on a snail's brown box.

The fountain eats moss, its source
a boss of leathery docks. Here
and there, lavender
and pale green leaves bush,
their buds stuck with cuckoo-spit.
And everywhere vetch and bindweed
puzzle and twist.

Days close on cauls of webs,
cadenzas of twitterings, then
cat's eyes, sudden among inky shadows.
Where hart's-tongue whiskers the cob-wall
and the ivy reaches thicken,

the glasshouse frame sinks
to its bed of smashed glass.

And out there, beyond that wall,
in the high-rise, the plastic world,
the great earth-eaters rear
with monstrous jaws, poised
to consume, consume.

TURNING POINT

Tap-dance lesson shows me time is motion:
it is never to stay still.
My new red shoes, like seed beans jumping
inside their bag, hungry for
the music of my feet,
I am first in Miss O'Hara's big bare room
to raise the piano lid, set records out.

When the older girls burst in, smug
behind lips tinted plum or coral,
we younger ones must practise,
'in the corner, please, last week's
shuffle-ball-flat-twirl-and-twirl'.

However hard I try,
I can't forget the school knickers I still wear,
long, navy-blue and thick.

And now the big girls,
in scant blue skirts and tops, are lining up
all set to attempt that new routine
they've seen perfected by the Royalettes,
and the keyboard warms
to Miss O'Hara's long red fingertips.

Slowly, it starts, then, I watch
their united skill and confidence let feet
automatically
tap out that rhythm mine still balk at.

Arms rest lightly on each other's hips,
heads bold above chiffon throats, breasts pointed;

then, right, front, lift, swing left, legs kick
thigh high for adolescent heats'
swirl to incense the air.

Transfixed, out of tune and slumped
in the corner, I am staring
at the flushed efforts of these intent
and future chorus girls:
I see their white thin briefs stained pink,
their stretched blue armpits sweated through.

FORCES

Unleashed, hostile, the wind came.
Its bayings had this house
like a signboard, creaking and slamming,
all night out on the hill. It whipped

chimneypots like spinning-tops,
and tackled slates like a team of
arm-wrestlers in enforced residence.
The wind pushed windowpanes trembling

into bedrooms, letting the sleet
flush us from our dreamy blue
to a gun-grey habitation. Powerless,
we watched the wind maul the beech tree

and lash out at the silver birch. Where
ivy clutched grey ash bark, the wind
paused; whetted lacquered claws to savage
the trellis and bleed rosebuds. It reared

to gnaw the yew tree then, spat it out
bottle green. The wind harried
and snapped at the washline till
the flustered reds, yellows and blues

flopped like rag dolls in the wet. Far up,
rooks, gulls were its crazed trapeze act.
We could not stand near the wind.
It beat our heads and shoved us back.

Our eyeballs stung from its fierce slap.
We feared this wind had come to get us.

It seemed nothing, man-made or mortal,
was safe in its manic attack. Except,

lodged in our glasshouse, all flesh,
the freshly decked Nelly Moser stood
untouched, in all her wide-eyed pink,
and observed this crude performance.
                                    Remote, calm.
A pale, thin, delicate lady.

FOR THIS DAY

Today her soft room gleams behind
windows pushed wide
on to a sky that is stretched
to the limit of its blue;
along the hedge bob sun-struck daffodils
excited by each other's gold.
She hugs this joy warily – a fragile thing,
or unmeant gift, which might be snatched away.

Downstairs, routine kitchen sounds
are roots of the ordinary day
and, in pubescent chaos,
her children shave the springy grass
to within an inch of its newfound life.
From high delicate branches a blackbird
splits the ether with its song.
The air is linen-fresh.

All round her this brute life thrusts:
its hormones, heartbeats, the swell
of tender buds dares her
to forget the unriddable – the quick
cold hands, cold words
dropped in those textbook rooms; clever
death's hungry probe
down the blood to where she is now,
contained in an unsweet discipline …

Know each blossoming to be the emblem
of survival and the reprieve
alive in that doctor's candid eyes
and for this day
unclinch.
Let go this pain.
Blink at its wet-winged giddy flight.

WASTELAND

You gave us the solid stuff of living:
early rising, well-brushed teeth
and hair, kitchen skills, needlework,
the rhythm of sown seed; facts
kept warm in a brown hen's clutch
and, at each day's start and finish, prayer.

We knew that Sunday silk and a tilted straw
was not a fancy to mask
the ordinary life, or soften
the conviction in your deeper self,
but a ploy of symmetry
you used in your need to remain afloat.

I watched you, wretched in double tragedy,
stay upright on your rock of hope
though wave after mountainous wave
of sorrow should have unmade you.
When that force engulfed me it was your
strength supported my sinking spirit.

Staunch mother
who had to re-learn long days unaided
but for safe activity and prayer;
I admire your courage. Now my life
seems empty of all those things I knew
I invoke deft hand, resolute mind
to come as lodestar to this narrowed waste.

A LIFE

for Jane

Were you the swelled bodice moist with milk;
bowlsful of brown eggs on a yellow tabletop,
buttermilk bread, the jacket on floury potatoes?

Were you the icing on a cake melted
into one summer birthday;
the magician of the treadle,
a drawer full of useless things?

Were you the dark mornings of the Nine Fridays,
the flowered straw at the evening meet;
the hard grey eyes of temper,
the hands of silk on well-soaped limbs?

Were you the cold holy water thrown after poltergeist,
the hot, china teapot flung in a rage;
the fierce pride of a slammed door,
the open hand to the hungry child?

Were you the tissue paper on flapper's finery,
the outraged at Hollywood's latest;
the lamp's-glow mothing children,
the ceaseless care of the aged?

Were you the art of living
clinched in that brittle diminishing round ...

You are a sprig of rosemary at a wake,
You are a handful of clay on a coffin lid.

CHRISTENING ROBE

The bundle, like a soft toy,
slipped from the top shelf,
concealed in haste

the day before I left the hospital.
Unfolding its expectant newness,
I imagine your head cusped

in dark down above this
loosed froth of lace,
your face pink and puckering

as the priest pours your name
over you. Startled, your hands
windmill a breath away

from my heart. My mind
swells as I fumble with slippery
ribbons, lay handfuls of lace

over putto feet. When I gather
you close, from somewhere deep
comes a low, long cry.

VAN GOGH'S ROOM IN ARLES

Night room we see by day:
where shadow is suppressed
and colour
does everything to penetrate
our defence against reality.

This is his way of creating
a calm, of reaching
into peace, of making a place
other to escape the violent world
he suffers.

And these flat washes furnish –

A few portraits on pale violet walls,
red floor-tiles, green window, lilac
doors; a blue jug upon an orange table.
The broad, fresh-buttery yellow
line of bed and chairs, and everywhere
the light
            striking
clean colours that soothe.

This is his new dreamed-of room:
with each coherent space the imagination's
nirvana.
            In this room nothing
is shuttered.

We watch this unique harmony of simple things.
Our minds at rest.
                        We wait.

And when he comes
                    dizzy
from the suction of the turnsole sun,
the black despair of cypresses, mute writhings
that are olive trees, that fireball rush
of stars,
          to throw

his shuddering, misfit body
onto the lemon-green cool sheets, we know
his burning head will flame,
                              become again
that fierce, first blaze,
                          the first
rotating sunflower.

AUBADE FOR A SCHOOLBOY

To come into your room
to find your dark head
sloped back on blue pillows
soft-snoring, your glasses
firm on your nose, automobile
catalogues, with fantastic

calculations and notes
in the margin, dropped
near you, strange music
drifting to the ceiling,
I know you are cruising
under the fixed stars

in your red mini-car
over remote desert sands,
or heedless of time,
tinkering in the greased
mysteries under a sleek
vintage-type bonnet:

how can I wake you
to the drabness of this
boxed-in life before
you glimpse one streak
of slivery dawn or
know the thrust and speed
of your own power?

A MIDDLING DAY

Under unbearable blue, today,
the beach lay tucked white
with emptied shells. The sea
inhaled, exhaled, wearied
by so many deaths. In the pale
shallows the children squealed and ran
tearing up the salt lace. Overhead,
low convoys of shorebirds flew
above the caravans to where fields
stirred, husk-green, deep as water;
and the birdscare gave out dull thuds
all day, like distant bombs.

Now the tide is on the turn, and
people have crunched back
to the swollen dunes, drifting
up the sandy slopes to the flicker
and pulse of summer homes, to shape
the hot night into those dreams
the flesh topples. Into a sky
plunged in mystery the white moon rides;
the one sleepless eye, watchful,
after this middling day, of the sea's
drag on its silver rein, this silted
head, this blood thinning.

BLUES

This room smacks
of a familiar mood. Stale
curtains droop; the corners
dim in conspiracy
of winter accomplices –
those brash magazines thrown
among the poetry and hardbacks;
the promises, promises of
holiday brochures sink
into a wreckage of bumf.

The wardrobe wallows
in its own mid-
life crisis. Nothing fits
on coathangers or in drawers.
The heavy door gapes
on the sad bulge of misfit
impulse buys and, worn once,
a ball-gown slumped
in a purple-dark sulk.

Outdoors, the heaped sky holds
no hope. Beneath the smog
the world is grey
on grey. Yet, it must
be spring – there, by the path,
a crocus thrusts, and something
pernickety
as instinct shifts and warns
it is time to straighten up.
To untack the cobwebs,
push the windows wide.

Let in the music that floats
from the tangle of the beech,
where, in the queer light,
a blackbird lords it in full throat.

THORN

How can I grasp this dream; this bine
that seeds from ditch to ditch, greens
hedgerows, riots colour down the glens,
shapes blood-ripe berries for a world
beyond this body, so exquisitely contrived
for pain, snapped from the probe
and force of sterile steel I wake to.

Always, blooming, I am there ahead
of quick cold hands that pry
into the secret chapters of the flesh,
words, dropped like stones to rattle
down the brain's incline. Leaping,
on the giddy slopes, I thrust
into the bright, unbroken blue.

The breeze is a song of fragrance;
flower jewels, small miracles of life,
blaze up, tantalise me. There I lose
ground, turn to find the way back
obstructed with monstrous growths.
Now in darkness, every hill's an ogre
set to pounce. On tangled briers

I bleed flesh, and now my footing's
gone, slow fall until at a scream's sound
this body lies still where pain winces
off dim walls. The mind again begins
its hypodermic calm. Am I wrong
to want a dream, vigorous and wild,
grafted to the moment of awakening.

ULSTER ELEMENT

That time the telegram arrived,
you dumb at its words, confounding me
with a grandmother's existence and death –
'Are we, or not, to attend her funeral?'

And I search your face, wanting to find
a tear, a quiver, anything to open
these floodgates to your past
where I might float secure on my own story.
But your body is chiselled stone.
I circle, closely, Mother's tears and prayers,
aware of stirrings out-fathoming her grief.

A second telegram states: 'Immediate
interment stop remains oedematous stop'.

They bury her without us near Strabane:
and I am the child who strains both ear and mind
to weave into the thin tapestry of my life
this Presbyterian woman stiff with pride
who'd spent her lifetime swallowing bitter tears,
to bulk it now with this waterlogged grandmother.

I grasp, in fear, the edge of this dark fact
and sense such order must be the will of things.
Her money changes nothing. Makes no waves,
turns no tides. The severing silence of years
still defines its border round our lives.

Christmas, years later, your head bent sipping port,
you seem unable to dam the blinding sadness
spilling into your glass and you turn,

in a harsh aside to me,
'She was as hard as nails you know',
and deftly you down your tear-charged drink.

A BACKWARDS LOOK

It is strange the way I used to think
my centuries-old and hip-thatched kitchen,
deep in the back of the house,
shut me in from the world,
hived me into its poverty –
how each small window doled out the light
in grimed swatches. A puzzle
of sky and rooftops I jigsawed
from sink to dresser to stove.

Strange, because now in this brand-new,
green and oak-trimmed room, bathed
in the shine of picture windows,
where I desert
my brood, the pots, this day
to lean on the bright glass and gaze;
the hardness and chill against my skin
carries me into an abandoned place,
a state of mind in which I clearly see …

Light reflected from the stable wall
knife into the cobbled alley;
where sad women-shapes
hung with sharp-faced children
peer from the smoke-filled cottages;
where sullen men stumble out to spit
and piss at the moon, where strays
prowl and watch
to scavenge the thickening stench.

OLIVER MARSHALL

Oliver Marshall was born in Clonmel, County Tipperary, in 1948. He was awarded an MA by University College Dublin in 1970. His poetry has appeared in *Rostrum, Poetry Ireland, Riverine* and *Irish Times*, and his three plays *Fantasia in the Dark, Happy Ever After* and *Remains* have been performed on RTE radio. He is the librarian in the Department of Education in Dublin.

FATHER'S DAY

I think of you,
Not as you were
The last Sunday
We met,

Eyes wet
As a child,
Hair this way and that
Like distraught grass.

What time is Mass?
You ask,
For the one hundredth time,
And Jesus, I can't wait

To get away from the weight
Of it all, wishing
I could be
Your child again

Under huge September moons.
But I stand my ground,
Soothe you as best I can.
The afternoon breathes

Mayflowers, trees,
A protection of mountains
Under a mature sky.
I kiss you goodbye,

Drive happily home that same
Landscape of black fields,

And amber lights strung out
Like Post Office twine,

Not caring that soon
It will be my turn
To stand
In the front line.

A TEA-CHEST OF BUNTING

to my father

Once a year
My father took home a tea-chest of bunting.
It sat like an abandoned birdcage near
The mahogany-stained shelves of silver my golfing
Grandaunt won in 1926, Shanghai,
Until the night before the Corpus Christi procession.
I held the ladder while he slung them high,
Poletop to poletop in a zigzag benediction
Of colour, a Dionysian stage-cloth of blues, reds, yellows, and
    lime-
Greens, a tutti of autumn migrants
Congregating two months before their time
To salute the rosary-covered elephant
Of the procession, caterpillar with a thousand feet
Throatrattling hosanna along the tar-perspiring street.

Each night I write
In my prison-windowed study, selfconsciously watching
A moon like a lost eucharist in flight
Between funereal poplars, I think of the tea-chest of bunting;
I wish I could snakecharm words from its mouth, fountain-
    high
In an arpeggio of pizzicato-pink pennants
Cat-arching the black-chasubled sky:
Ciborium-gold, regatta-red, snow pallor –
I wish all Ireland might queue like communicants
Before my kitetails of triangular colour.

UNCLES

*In memory of Francis and Christopher Marshall, drowned on a
Clonmel Post Office outing to Clonea, August 5th, 1951*

I never saw you drown.
All my childhood you smiled from the wall like saints,
Your faces flushed by the photographer's rouge.
Frankie and Christy. But for the sadness, the names
Could have chimed well on a billboard over the Oisín,
Or tucked under ten-shilling notes in birthday cards
To relations you never saw.

Drowned at Clonea, August 5th, 1951 ...
Sunday after Sunday until I was twelve
I wiped the birdshit from your gravestone,
Or knelt bare-kneed beside my father,
Uncertain whether to pray to you or for you;
Guilty that in secret I was glad
You, not he, were dead.

I had a hold of their hands, Oliver, only a wave ...
But for a grandaunt I would have missed the funeral,
Though I remember only black coats, faces, silence.
*Not one word was spoken on the way
Over or on the way back,* my mother said; but
It is easy to imagine the grief: young
Trees summery on The Mall, a twelve-foot grave.

I have to look at a map to remember the way:
Newcastle, Clogheen, The Vee ... At Melleray
You stand for your last photograph. You look happy.
Back in the bus, I imagine you up front, laughing,
Or wondering (townies) if the yellow fields were oats or
   barley,

Or counting the days to your wedding (Christy) or The Final
    (Frankie);
But maybe you sat like my parents, unspeaking, at the back.

Beyond Dungarvan you lean out to clean your heads
Of placenames that every day cling like dust to your
Black uniforms: Marlfield, Mountain Lodge, Scrouthea ...
Then, flashing like a knife in the sun, Clonea.
You are too long dead for me to mourn,
And now I no longer pray. But I can hold
You here undrowned for ever, hands

Lifted in my father's hands, above the waves.

'You won't be going to school today'
Was how my father told me she died.
He stood in my bedroom doorway

Holding a tear-damp handkerchief.
His mother. I hardly knew her,
But I understood the grief:

Four months before, September,
My own mother was ambulanced away
And hadn't yet come back. I remember

Going to see her once, geraniums
Tinting the skin-coloured walls
Of a now-defunct sanatorium.

I think she smiled and said hello,
But that was all.
It seemed years ago

I followed her in fields above
The town, hoping
For random handfuls of love.

Years later she told my wife
These months from home
Were among the happiest of her life.

All winter my father and I kept
Mournful company. And now his
Own mother was dead, he wept

And pushed me into the black
Room where she lay
Like Rawalpindi ice-stroked on its back.

I stood in terror, bands
Of perspiration breaking out like fire:
I touched her subzero hands.

Two weeks later I didn't care
That she was dead. I knew
My own mother was still there.

I left my father on his own,
And wore my black diamond to see
Gregory Peck in *The Guns of Navarone*.

In the spring, my own mother
Came home. Her coat was red, but
Her hands were like March weather.

JOE

You came each year for Christmas,
Sleigh-riding through Wexford and Waterford
Like a second-class Santa Claus on the old *Rosslare*.
My mother's only brother ...

My father is hardly at the Convent Bridge,
Parcels hanging like turkeys from the handlebars
Of his black Post Office bike, as I rise
And carefully stow my dreams under a pillow
Persil-white as the hills in my window,
And runwalk Gallows Hill to meet the train,
Dropping size-five wellington prints
Like litter in the ankle-high snow.

In the winterdark station where
My grandfather queued for the First World War,
A single red light burns – the signal.
It is like a country chapel waiting for a funeral:
Taximen stamp their feet like undertakers,
Cough Craven A, Sweet Afton and Woodbine coughs,
Speculate how much the Fishguard boat is late.
'Go home out of that, you friggin' Arab,'
One shouts for a laugh,
Spotting my queer-shaped, bilious-coloured plastic raincap.
Blushing, I furl my frightened snail antennae,
And weigh myself in hundredweights –
Or climb the iron bridge to peep
Through its Meccano-set bars
On Clonmel lying-on for second sleep –
Until the red light turns to green,
And the lighted carriages feed like rapid cinematic images
Before my timid astigmatic eyes.

'Hello, Oliver.'
I turn to see you stand,
An apparition in steamsmoke, holding out your hand;
Then sit behind you on the cushioned back
Of Bernie Keane's black hackney,
Gliding like King Faisal through hankywhite air:
The Railway to 2 Queen Street,
A huge five-shilling fare.

Your suitcase opens like Ali Baba's cave,
Dazzling my impatient after-breakfast gaze:
Photographs (black-and-white Ilford 120) of the
    coronation,
Air-displays flying like fireworks
Over pompous Elizabethan days; autographs:
Gene Autry, Sir Edmund Hillary, Max Bygraves ...
For a small-town child, it was a magnificent bazaar,
An anthology of free magician fairs: jars
Of pomade, purchased in a Tipperary accent –
'Surely you mean Morgan's *Pomawd*, sir?' –
The first trousers-press in Ireland for my father;
The statue of Eros in miniature; a barometer
I broke by holding to the fire
To see how high the mercury would climb;
Chopsticks, dominoes, trick cards, a cricket bat,
And a gasometer-shaped coil of wire
That laboured like a rheumatic cat
Down the fifteen steps of our uncarpeted stairs.

You were married in the hot September
Of 1959, three days before I was eleven. On
Mill Hill Broadway, in your monkey suit and thinning hair,
You were like a convert at a First Communion,
A small boy answering the door to love.
Afterwards, you hardly ever came. I remember

A postcard to my mother from Pontin's:
'Here for a day on my own. No one else would come …'

Last time we met
I drove through the Blackwall Tunnel
With an unhappy wife and a crying child
To Edgware General Hospital, where your own wife
Lifts her lollipop like a useless monstrance
Over secular London's unending traffic. It
Seemed time was a second-hand hat
Turned inside out, that
I was the uncle, you the child.

Once this summer, locked like Houdini inside
An ice-thick depression I cannot crack, I said:
'I want to end this troubled marriage.'
That night you came into the coffin-tight
Bedroom of my mobile home, flying
Around and around above my head
Like a battery-controlled redundant postman,
Your empty mailbags
Miraculously dispensing love.

THE KING'S SHILLING

In memoriam FCM, *d. 1937*

I seem to imagine the whole thing
Like the beginning of a Hardy novel:
November 1886. *Fin-de-siècle* rings
Of light loop Kilkenny roofs and hovels
As you set out to take the King's
Shilling. Thirty miles away, Clonmel

Waits like a woman for a blind date.
But perhaps it was August, and miles
Outside the town you piss into a gate,
While wind skis zigzag through walls
Of coffin-coloured corn. Above, fate
Shakes open like a scarf: Taj Mahal,

Where my father first found his face
In a pool of goldfish; Rawalpindi,
Dressed like a bride in Rajah lace;
Or, a century later, a tiny Sindy
Doll loved by my child in a place
You never saw, Portobello. Dingy

Streets near Black Abbey were your
First home, a mother held you in her
Shadow. On a table near the parlour
Door you wrote in quill: *Mother,*
I'm going to Clonmel. I may never
See you again, Francis. Other

Images of flight come; but afraid
To amplify your life with mine,

37

I plot your journey in my head:
Callan, where you knock nine
Pints of cider cleanly dead
Like skittles; Killamery; Nine

Mile House, where you fall asleep
And hear her sad voice cry
Come back, Francis. But you keep
Going until churchspires rise high
Like pencils into Clonmel's deep
Red and satsuma-tinted sky.

WAITING FOR EASTER

I held your hands in mine
The day we were married,
Kneeling to bread and wine
We no longer believed

In; prayed we would survive
Faith-crisis in our love.
Years later, as we strived
To save ourselves above

Open-jawed hells of hate,
I saw your hands wave to
Love's purgatorial gate,
Hoped we might survive two

Night-years of marital
Lent, when the velours-
Fleeced white nuptials
Of any love but ours

Were imagination's
Goal. Not till Easter –
Sun-dance salvation
Of daffodils in cluster –

Comes (though I woke last night
To find your hands glove-tight in
Mine, a million ice-white
Volts of love within

Your ring) will I know if life
Can mouth-kiss love revived

For us as man or wife;
And if we have survived.

MIDDLE-AGE IN KERRY

I wasn't aware of your needs:
You were too aware of mine. Half the night
My mind tries to find some comforting seeds

Of meaning for this harsh catastrophe.
I grope for the unfamiliar light-switch,
Go barefooted to make a cup of tea

To have with this dryly-crumbling fruitcake
You made for my thirty-seventh birthday.
Like an ironic gesture at our wake,

Wind sings a lugubrious wedding-song
Above these four-square, stone-divided fields,
And look – there at the bottom of the long

Garden where my sister will sow sweet thyme
And skin-soft roses, our red Renault waits
Like a hearse, thirty years before its time.

ISLINGTON AVENUE

There's little here to make one write.
Chaste-walled bedroom of this small flat,
That suitcase where you packed your whites

Twenty years ago this autumn
And waited, nun-protected, for
The future to break its hymen.

Nothing happens in this empty
Present. A hundred miles away,
Dreaming of unhappiness, my

Father takes his time to die. I
Think of you alone in our big
Bedroom, and wonder again why

We cannot be here together,
Making love, undiscouraged by
This dying October weather.

But love, like death, can take its time
To manufacture an order.
We can only wait for its slime-

Wreathed garland to fall our way.
Outside, I can hear nothing but
That dismal foghorn bay

Pain-widening rings down this long night,
A tired dinosaur waking from
Sleep, into arrow-hurting light.

LES DERNIERS HIVERS D'UN ANCIEN ACTEUR DES PAROLES

for Philip Larkin

Alone in a house whose rooms
Of sepia resemble
Tombs in an Italian cemetery –
His grandfather, sitting in the first
Car in Tipperary; his parents,
Smiling in their wedding-suits
A year before the War – he thinks for the millionth time
Of Pavese's last despairing cry:
Non scrivero più.

Each morning, depression
Sits like a pigeon on his head;
He tries to make it lift; it
Sits deeper, now a crown of thorns.
In the garden, final roses drop
Their heads (in crimson and vermilion coincidence);
A child's trike waits like a lost
Suitcase for its owner; and high
Above a neighbour's roof, ghostly poplars

Shimmer like a woman's tresses
In a summer river. Words,
Always the same – *father, mother,*
Childhood, love – begin like tumours in his brain,
Or fester like worms in a fisherman's cup;
It would take a surgeon's scalpel
Years to cut them free.
He walks from room to room.
Sentences lie on chairs

Like unfinished knitting. *In 1957,*
At the age of nine, I pick
Windfalls with my father
In a dying garden. Our fingers touch ...
Four years later, in my mother's
Pink handmirror, I search anxiously
For my whiskered, androgynous face ...
At night he dreams
He is the boy Mozart,

All Europe – Paris, Mannheim, Wien –
Minuetting like toys
To the tinkling of his holy hands;
But wakes instead to find
His own hands crossed, as if
Old Nurse Hunt has parachuted in from childhood
To prepare his last (unanointed) evening.
He rises, dons the brown
Dressing-gown, that (hooded)

Makes him look like Friedrich's monk.
He tries to write (or shit words); fails.
Falling asleep, he dreams
In hate the moon
Is a mad Gestapo searchlight
Tormenting the ruins of his once beautiful
Eighteenth-century city. Once, too,
Words came like birds from his sleeve.
Now, old artificer, stauncher, *maestro delle belle parole,*
He has forgotten how.

PIED PIPER

to Emily

The whole thing
Is a huge lie:
He lured you
Not with watery
Piping, but with
Words – not words
That lay about
Your lives like
Home-made toys:
Grossvater or
Grossmutter or
Heilige Nacht –
But weird words
You never heard:
Fire and *earth*
And *nightsky*
And *woodwind;*
Corkscrew you
Loved, but
Thistlefunnel
Was the funniest;
He tossed it
In the air,
Pancake-high;
Not even when it
Smashed in splinters
At your clog-encumbered feet
Did you suspect
Anything was wrong –
Not until you

Came to the thyme-
Covered cave where
He drowned you all
In the Niagara Falls
Of his rhymes.

THREE DAYS' DARKNESS

to John McGahern

When I was seven,
The Irish Catholic
Said that Heaven
And its apocalyptic
Joys were on their way:
Three days' darkness
Would squat like stray
Tenants on the fastness
Of our holy land.
Penance would fill the hours
To stay the stern hand
Of God above the fires
Of Hell. Candles would refuse
To burn in the homes
Of mortal sinners or Jews –
Thus we'd know the names
Of those bound for the far
Side of Christ. I kissed
My medals and scapulars,
Afraid I had missed
Heaven by my silly
Act: in Doctor Murphy's garden
I pulled down the frilly
Knickers of a maiden,
And swooned in polymorphous
And O yes intense
Joy on the amorphous
Miniature kiss
Of a future mayoress.
Heaven never came,

Despite the stress
Of waiting. The game
Of eschatology
Was easily revealed
For the codology
It was. Congealed
Lives flowed again
Along familiar rivers
Of dull routine. Rain
Fell like unwanted slivers
Of sanctifying grace
On sun-forgotten summers
In laurelled Brighton Place.
Busby-headed drummers
Led Patrick's Day parades –
There were accordion-chested
Mummers, childish escapades
In Troy's tree-infested
Shades – but not the long
Procession past our sill
To join the black throng
Of travellers on Gallows Hill –
Clonmel's bleeding vein
Of nightly emigration.
The nearest I ever came
To divine salvation
Was when my father,
His arms akimbo,
Told my mother
He'd located Limbo
On our small Pye
Electric wireless –
I heard the souls cry
In darkness that was fireless –
Or when with Jackie Ahearne

I ran down to greet
Sputnik 1 as it turned
The corner of Queen Street,
Tacking close to Heaven,
On the 5th October, 1957.

THE GHENT ALTARPIECE

to Renée Parsons

You do not begin
With geometric calculation
À l'italienne,
Nor with soprano variation
Of colour
À l'allemande,
But with quiet prayer:
Que Dieu m'aide, un flamand,
À achever cette peinture –
Then the calm
Miniature
Scrape of psalmy
Colour on the King
Of Heaven's cloth –
Hear how it sings,
Crimson-deep moth.

Citizens of Ghent
Swap unhappiness
Like so many bent
Coins in the darkness
Which you illuminate
Like a manuscript:
Eve's aberrant
Thighs and Pict-
Sized genitalia
You easily execute –
Simple paraphernalia
Of this holy act –
Saving, I note,

Your most precious oils
For the pendulous weight
Of Adam's balls.

Four summers ago
I saw an old man
Turn the slow
Time-pocked panels
Before my agnostic
Eyes – now one side,
Now another, fantastic
Oeuvre of Jan van Eyck
And Hubert his older
Brother – and wished I
Was less colder
In my faith, that Heaven's sky
Could muster a parade
Of light to outsummer
This magnificent man-made
Sacrament of colour.

YOU

They said You died
Especially for me:
Good Friday, wide-
Armed on a tree.

I spent my child-
Hood loving You,
Night on prayer-wild
Night; but did You

Once give my love
Satisfaction?
My father drove
To distraction

Babbling to You
An unhappy life;
Celibate Jew,
Why didn't his wife

Love him better?
You tied my family
In ice-lined fetters
With your homily,

Blind pilgrimage
Standing in for
Faith-strong marriage.
Year after year

Religious rites
Wound their tails

Like altar-kites
Around my sail –

Full faith. Did this
Bring happiness,
Heaven-high bliss,
More close? O yes,

Age-coloured grief
Came in plane-low
Above the fief-
Held town below

The mountains (river,
Canopy of cloud,
Turned the colour
Of full-brown shroud

The day my uncles died).
You were always
There when Death cried
In small hallways

On our street. Why
Did You not once
Come down and try
To turn the advance

Of time? Why were
Organ-throbbing
Chapels (air
Funeral-sobbing)

Full of candle-
Guarded cold Death?

You turned the handle
Of warm Life's breath-

Arresting wheel. Kindle
Faith's miracle
In my spindle-
Held tabernacle

Of hate. Mould
My thurible
Of lead to gold –
If you're able.

FAITH, HOPE AND CHARITY

I do not know what colour faith is:
A soul-white persistence of limestone
Through centuries of dark, rock-hard like bone
Or a child's belief in Santa Claus,

Perhaps. Charity could be red as fire
Or measles, a candle-flame to warm the hands
Of women looting earth-crops in ice-webbed lands,
Warm as cow-breath in a winter byre.

But hope I think I certainly know:
Miles and miles of juniper plant
Mole-heading the darkness like an ant,
Coil-springing its green-head above the snow.

PATRICK RAMSEY

Patrick Ramsey was born in New Jersey in 1962.
He came to Northern Ireland in 1970 and was
educated there at St Peter's Secondary School and
Queen's University Belfast. His work has appeared
in *Riverine, Gown Literary Supplement, North Dakota
Review* and has been read on BBC Radio Ulster. He
works in publishing.

A SONG FOR APPRENTICES

Dejected, knowing my rhymes
Have been minted more freshly
So many countless times

And my each and every metaphor
Has been worked more deftly
A thousand times before

By better poets, better men,
Firmly grounded in their craft,
I think once again

Of Fats and Jelly Roll,
How they read like blind men
From a worn mechanical scroll

The Brailled genius of other masters,
The maestros of bordello rags,
And how they sensed their failures

With a despairing unease,
Their fingers ineptly matching
A mentor's handwork, his ghost keys.

UPON HEARING DYLAN THOMAS'S POETRY
DESCRIBED AS CARELESS

Hard to think of you any other way
But smashed, on all fours, your ruined life astray,
Intoxicated on plush words, bad booze,
Filled with Welsh melancholy, Celtic blues,
The last poet to live out our last myth
Of the poet, the muse-taunted wordsmith.

Yet I think of it but as your public face.
Or rather merely having the good grace
Of preserving the correct perspective,
Keeping the artist, the work, distinctive,
Not inviting the eager public – us! –
To view your workroom, your seashaken house.

Notebooks, worksheets, show you industrious,
Hacking the rumpus of shapes, studious
In your way; criss-crossed pages, altered proofs,
The basis of all your inspired truths.
I see you crafting the syllables, the rhymes,
Into ordered phalanxes, singing lines.

INTO THE BLUE:
AN IMPROMPTU ELEGY FOR GEORGE BUCHANAN

Your legacy, an aesthetic –
Enabling – that we can live by,
Mistrusting the old rhetoric,
The cold institutional lie,

Of the statesman and priest, to dent
Apathy and indifference
With nothing but the fixed dissent
Of idealism, common sense,

A faith in open-mindedness,
The moment's controlled collision,
Its swift dynamic synthesis;
The humane and social vision

Of not living in the past, its hate,
But in the here-and-now; to see
The better future, anticipate
The people that we may well be,

Working towards that new city
Of clean progress, sunlit parks,
And each accepting each – pretty
Girls, old maids, artists, heroes, clerks –

Lounging without shame on cut grass,
Tough and mortal, mindful, active,
Blazing particles of the mass
Making existence attractive.

It's a kind of dogma, no doubt,
But a good one. A lore of civics
Towards the necessary breakout,
Ways of outstaring your cynics.

UPON READING *THE SELECTED JOHN HEWITT*

As always, the sombre, austere tone. Calm
Invigilator, your painter's eye a tact
For a plain truth; the look and word exact,

As steady, as deft, as the draftsman's arm;
Each stroke distinct; no curve, no *wristy trick*;
No flatterer of our gruff local charm;

The observer of a tight-lipped rhetoric.

FOR CERTAIN POETS

Your gift, not how to live, but how to see
The unnerving, fruitful conspiracy

Of common things: journeys, hurried letters,
Shopping, sniping at your literary betters,

Your liking for Scotch whisky, jazz and blues,
Or standing appalled at the latest news,

You depict this crass yet wonderous age
With quiet markings upon the blank page

Spoken with a tempered, a restrained voice,
Teaching man not just to sorrow, but rejoice.

Life has good things. Show them to the light!
Ideas pulled carefully like a kite,

Thrown to the heavens yet strung to earth
By the old subjects: love, death, a child's birth,

Crafted naturally with the poet's art
To find their echoes in the reader's heart.

By praising the good book, that woman's fuss,
You add to the clutter of each lived-in house ...

5.40. Struggling out of my office,
I think of you, the last true Parisian,
There in your attic room, the prints of
Matisse and Chagall not quite flush
On the walls yellow with damp and steam.
From a corner, in breathy mono, Dex's
Hanging his tears out to dry, making
Even the whatnots weep with the sheer
Fittingness of it all.
                            And you,
Under the sheets, listening, perhaps,
To her heart's sleep-filled beating,
Like accents over your latest poem.

And, to be honest, I think I could
Clutch my ulcer in a rictus of
Pure, wholesome jealousy at this,
As Larkin would say, version of a life,
Reprehensible, perfect.

REVISIONIST

for Gail

Re-writing this, our history, films
Have been spliced, edited
In a somewhat arbitrary fashion, still
Photos re-touched, the archives raided.
Certain tapes have been erased.

Yet I, the historian, the trained censor,
Am not too happy with the finished job,
Or rather the first drafts,
The first explanations of what happened.
Too many odds and ends,

Acts of inexplicable tenderness.

THE LONELY RETURNS TO THE LONELY

The fields always look desolate, bitter.
Mist sodden, hewn raw by cutting winds,
The hills are a sombre swathe of damp ferns.

On a secluded slope, the off-white cottage
Where she lies, a reticent fascination.

You want to lift the still, unyielding latch,
The drab twilight easing across whitened stone,
And see her sleeping, the fire turned to ash;

A wave of narcissi; the paraffin lamp,
Its tremulous flame, a severed blush,

The broken rachis of a peacock's feather.

LOVE POEM

A love so slight,
It was like rhyming 'dreams' with 'arms'.

Now, five or six years after,
I scan complacent crowds,
Listen for your unmapped laughter.

Despite all your protestations,
I knew you never wanted to figure in my poems.
So now – too late, I know – I imagine you
Striding purposefully through
The Saturday afternoon crowds
Of Castle Lane
Or Fountain Lane,
Your legs less fragile, more masculine,
Than once I liked to pretend.

RE-READING 'THE RIBBON'

As the city sleeps,
Clothed or unclothed in solitude,
I brood beneath your bedside lamp,

Say and re-say your name;
Your face; a scattering of memories;
The rhythms of your days with me ...

Cigarettes ... a whiskey glass ...
I listen to the radio's hiss,
And your absence settling in waves.

I have scattered your books across the floor.
I read once again
Such words, such sad truisms –

*It seems ridiculous
How everything acknowledges her touch ...*
As it will, the night wanes,

A residue of dream, disappointments.
And I think you were like a poem
Lost between the sense of longing,

The want of its articulation.

*from 'The Ribbon' by Hugo Williams

DRIVING THROUGH COUNTY MONAGHAN

'jazz   [a music] improvised on a given
harmonic sequence against a background of
clearly defined rhythm'
                    Fontana Dictionary of Modern Thought

Like the cat's-eyes' abstract light
on these dark and endless roads,
thoughts approach me,
ironies without context.

From the dashboard, a dull glow;
the rhythms of listless jazz
(blue notes – thirds and sevenths);
the swash of foreign stations.

Music and static ... distance –
a vague continuous wave
like the sway of tall grasses
across dank continental fields,

or the sea as it beats and falls
against white and unlikely coasts.

FLAT PROJECTIONS: JANUARY 1988

for Judith Jordan

I

It is winter. Li Ho
   or Tu Mu, perhaps,
      could have made something of this.
I can't.
   The mountain side
      above which
is the full moon,
   its wintered light
      and the New Year frost –
the slow contours,
   the thin uneven edges,
      the tints
of sapphire, of blue –
   like the lines, the shadings,
      of a too subtle cartographer.

II

Above, in the chill bitter wind,
   dark clouds scuttle,
the season early. While unseen
   and inexactly sensed,
the black unfathomable lough;
   its sudden white wounds
offered to the elements; the slow burning
   of lights in unlikely attics.

III

And there below,
   the city – what else? – sleeps,

empty,
whitening in mind
  like a parable of silence,
    oblivious
to the river's black running,
  once more, the first unsteady line
    upon the perfect page,
the page untouched.

AN AFTERNOON IN THE PARK

Another August day glides pointlessly on.
This, you know, is the hour no one likes –
Two to three o'clock. Thoughts grow unfocused.
The afternoon swelters. You wish to sleep
But cannot. In the mid-distance trees sway
In the gentle breeze. Beyond the park gates,
The traffic thins like the cries of children;
A silence, of sorts, listlessly settles.

From the empty municipal buildings
Idle light comes off glass. The minutes
Dawdle along the lashes of your eye;
You hear them singing their monotonous airs
Of mere infinity and nothingness,
Their old unambiguous ironies.

POEM OVERLOOKING BELFAST LOUGH

for David Trouton

Looking out, you dream of distant shores,
Of loves in foreign cities, to be free,
Shrug off the dull responsibility
Of house, job, wife and kids – domestic chores –

And start again with the ideals of youth,
Live on energy and raw nerve. Find you're
Alone once more, slightly soiled, insecure,
Yet on amicable terms with the truth –

Whatever *that* is. It's a useful dream
But that's all it is. The good life's here –
Both prospective and real. Your proper sphere
Lies in the rituals of hearth and home.

The secret's remaining flexible, skilled.
Like anywhere, *here* is a place to build.